O AME]

WHERE ART THOU?

By Rev. Jean-Paul Engler

INTRODUCTION

For a number of years, I have wanted to write a book about my experiences as an immigrant to the United States. But until recently, I did not feel the urgency to do so.

As a Christian minister born outside of America, who chose to live in what I perceived to be the greatest country on earth, I feel that I can bring a unique perspective on what is currently developing and on what is about to happen to our beloved nation.

The title of this book came to me as I was meditating on why my wife and I left our native country of France some 46 years ago. We knew very little about this new country that was to become our home. But one thing we were certain of, it couldn't be worse than the place we'd been born and raised in. Socialism had slowly but surely squeezed the life out of the country. Opportunities for advancement were quickly disappearing. And now today, I can't help but wonder what happened to the land of liberty, opportunity and respect for God we came to love almost half a century ago. Thus the question: O America, where art thou?

Of course, we could just reminisce about days gone by and wonder about what could have been, but that won't bring America back or slow down the downward spiral our beloved country has been on for the past few years. I believe that it is the responsibility of those who truly love this nation, to take a stand against anything or anyone that attempts to destroy it.

I'm sure that you have wondered, as I have, about the absence of any prophetic biblical reference to the United States of America in end-time events. While many other nations and kingdoms are mentioned, how could such a great and powerful country possibly be left out?

In this book, we will not only answer this important question, but we'll also find out what brought us here and what we can do to stop the enemies of this country from causing even more damage than they already have.

My ultimate goal, however, is to mobilize as many of God's people in this country, to take up their spiritual weapons and fight for the freedom that cost the lives of so many before us!

TABLE OF CONTENTS

CHAPTER 1

AMERICA, WHO ART THOU?

Before answering the question: "where is America today?", we must first establish who America is. Just as Israel has a unique identity and its people have a particular destiny in God, this nation and its people have been chosen by divine purpose.

Any criminal investigator will tell you that If one wants to establish the identity of a person in a definite way, DNA testing is the most conclusive method available today. As they go through the maturing process, both humans and nations, go through changes, but their DNA remains the same. I believe that if we want to determine who America really is, we must study it's origins. To successfully do that, all alterations and modifications to the original, must be ignored.

Do not remove the ancient landmark
Which your fathers have set.

Proverbs 22:28

Many are working hard to implement the failed socialist agenda of Europe in this country.

There is a deliberate effort on the part of liberals today, to do away with everything that once made America great. It was not the Founding Father's intention to reproduce what they fought so hard to free themselves from.

There are certain traits, characteristics and attributes that make America what it is. As "ancient landmarks" are consistently being moved and the very identity of America is being questioned, it is becoming increasingly difficult to recognize the wonderful nation God intended it to be.

To better understand what makes America special, we must first look at what prompted the Puritans to leave their native England. They had to brave treacherous seas to begin a new life in an unfamiliar setting. Of course they were fleeing the persecution from both the official religious establishment and from King James V, but most importantly, they wanted to have the freedom to practice their Christian faith and enjoy their God-given liberty.

The original documents of this nation were both statements of faith and defining bylaws meant to enable future generations to achieve these worthy goals contained therein.

AMERICA'S UNIQUE CARACTER

It's a mystery to me how anyone can deny that this country was built on Christian principles. Not only was this obvious to the founding fathers, but pretty much every President since George Washington felt mandated to maintain, uphold and implement this reality.

"The fundamental basis for this nation's laws was given to Moses on the Mount. The fundamental basis of our Bill of Rights comes from the teachings we get from Exodus and Saint Matthew, from Isaiah and Saint Paul....If we don't have a proper fundamental moral background, we will finally end up with a totalitarian government which does not believe in rights for anybody except the State!"

Harry Truman, 33rd President

Not only does America have a unique identity, but it was also entrusted with a vision and a God ordained destiny. For most of it's history, not only was our nation conscious of it's divine purpose, but it was deeply dedicated to its fulfillment.

"God's purpose for extracting the Children of Israel from Egypt was much more than a rescue mission. His ultimate goal for them, was to establish a nation that would be governed by God through the leadership of His choice and according to the principles He'd established. They were not merely asked to occupy a piece of real estate in the Middle East, they were to be a testimony for God to the entire region and to the world!"

Benjamin Harrison, 23rd President

Unfortunately, many people in leadership today, are unaware of this purpose and are consequently not engaged in its accomplishment. For the Apostle Paul to be obedient to the heavenly vision, he obviously had to first have a revelation of it.

"I was not disobedient to the heavenly vision"

Acts 26:19

From the moment the first settlers came to this land, they understood that their purpose for coming to this new land wasn't merely to flee religious persecution.

I am absolutely convinced that America was chosen by God, to fulfill a specific purpose on the earth and somehow, the pilgrims were keenly aware of it.

THE MAYFLOWER COMPACT

In the name of God, Amen. We, whose names are underwritten, the loyal subjects of our dread sovereigne Lord King James, by the grace of God, of Great Britaine, France, and Ireland king, defender of the faith, etc.

Having undertaken, for the glory of God, and advancement of the Christian faith, and honour of our king and country, a voyage to plant the first colony in the Northerne parts of Virginia, doe, by these presents, solemnly and mutually in the presence of God, and one of another, covenant and combine ourselves together into a civill body politick, for our better ordering and preservation and furtherance of the ends aforesaid; and by virtue hereof to enacte, constitute, and frame such just and equall laws, ordinances, acts, constitutions, and offices, from time to time, as shall be thought most meete and convenient for the general good of the Colonie unto which we promise all due submission and obedience. In witness whereof we have hereunder subscribed our names at Cap-Codd the 11, of. November, in the year of the raigne of our sovereigne Lord King James of England, France, and Ireland, the eighteenth, and of Scotland the fiftie-fourth. Anno. Dom. 1620.

This document was written by the first settlers and outlined what they believed to be the vision God gave them for the newly-settled territory.

*MAYFLOWER COMPACT -From the *History of Plymouth Plantation* by William Bradford (1590-1657), second governor of Plymouth.

*Note: All historical documents are printed in their original format.

THE DECLARATION OF INDEPENDENCE

IN CONGRESS, July 4, 1776.

The unanimous Declaration of the thirteen United States of America,

When in the Course of human events, it becomes necessary for one people to dissolve the political bands which have connected them with another, and to assume among the powers of the earth, the separate and equal station to which the Laws of Nature and of Nature's God entitle them, a decent respect to the opinions of mankind requires that they should declare the causes which impel them to the separation.

We hold these truths to be self-evident, that all men are created equal, that they are endowed by their Creator with certain unalienable Rights, that among these are Life, Liberty and the pursuit of Happiness.--That to secure these rights, Governments are instituted among Men, deriving their just powers from the consent of the governed, --That whenever any Form of Government becomes destructive of these ends, it is the Right of the People to alter or to abolish it, and to institute new Government, laying its foundation on such principles and organizing its powers in such form, as to them shall seem most likely to effect their Safety and Happiness. Prudence, indeed, will dictate that Governments long established should not be changed for light and transient causes; and accordingly all experience hath shewn, that mankind are more disposed to suffer, while evils are sufferable, than to right themselves by abolishing the forms to which they are accustomed. But when a long train of abuses and usurpations, pursuing invariably the same Object evinces a design to reduce them under absolute Despotism, it is their right, it is their duty, to throw off such Government, and to provide new Guards for their future security.--Such has been the patient sufferance of these Colonies; and such is now the necessity which constrains them to alter their former Systems of Government. The history of the present King of Great Britain is a history of repeated injuries and usurpations, all having in direct object the establishment of an absolute Tyranny over these States. To prove this, let Facts be submitted to a candid world.

He has refused his Assent to Laws, the most wholesome and necessary for the public good.
He has forbidden his Governors to pass Laws of immediate and pressing importance, unless suspended in their operation till his Assent should be obtained; and when so suspended, he has utterly neglected to attend to them.
He has refused to pass other Laws for the accommodation of large districts of people, unless those people would relinquish the right of Representation in the Legislature, a right inestimable to them and formidable to tyrants only.
He has called together legislative bodies at places unusual, uncomfortable, and distant from the depository of their public Records, for the sole purpose of fatiguing them into compliance with his measures.
He has dissolved Representative Houses repeatedly, for opposing with manly firmness his invasions on the rights of the people.
He has refused for a long time, after such dissolutions, to cause others to be elected; whereby the Legislative powers, incapable of Annihilation, have returned to the People at large for their exercise; the State remaining in the mean time exposed to all the dangers of invasion from without, and convulsions within.
He has endeavoured to prevent the population of these States; for that purpose obstructing the Laws for Naturalization of Foreigners; refusing to pass others to encourage their migrations hither, and raising the conditions of new Appropriations of Lands.
He has obstructed the Administration of Justice, by refusing his Assent to Laws for establishing Judiciary powers.
He has made Judges dependent on his Will alone, for the tenure of their offices, and the amount and payment of their salaries.
He has erected a multitude of New Offices, and sent hither swarms of Officers to harrass our people, and eat out their

substance.

He has kept among us, in times of peace, Standing Armies without the Consent of our legislatures.

He has affected to render the Military independent of and superior to the Civil power.

He has combined with others to subject us to a jurisdiction foreign to our constitution, and unacknowledged by our laws; giving his Assent to their Acts of pretended Legislation:

For Quartering large bodies of armed troops among us:

For protecting them, by a mock Trial, from punishment for any Murders which they should commit on the Inhabitants of these States:

For cutting off our Trade with all parts of the world:

For imposing Taxes on us without our Consent:

For depriving us in many cases, of the benefits of Trial by Jury:

For transporting us beyond Seas to be tried for pretended offences

For abolishing the free System of English Laws in a neighbouring Province, establishing therein an Arbitrary government, and enlarging its Boundaries so as to render it at once an example and fit instrument for introducing the same absolute rule into these Colonies:

For taking away our Charters, abolishing our most valuable Laws, and altering fundamentally the Forms of our Governments:

For suspending our own Legislatures, and declaring themselves invested with power to legislate for us in all cases whatsoever.

He has abdicated Government here, by declaring us out of his Protection and waging War against us.

He has plundered our seas, ravaged our Coasts, burnt our towns, and destroyed the lives of our people.

He is at this time transporting large Armies of foreign Mercenaries to compleat the works of death, desolation and tyranny, already begun with circumstances of Cruelty & perfidy scarcely paralleled in the most barbarous ages, and totally unworthy the Head of a civilized nation.

He has constrained our fellow Citizens taken Captive on the high Seas to bear Arms against their Country, to become the executioners of their friends and Brethren, or to fall themselves by their Hands.

He has excited domestic insurrections amongst us, and has endeavoured to bring on the inhabitants of our frontiers, the merciless Indian Savages, whose known rule of warfare, is an undistinguished destruction of all ages, sexes and conditions.

In every stage of these Oppressions We have Petitioned for Redress in the most humble terms: Our repeated Petitions have been answered only by repeated injury. A Prince whose character is thus marked by every act which may define a Tyrant, is unfit to be the ruler of a free people.

Nor have We been wanting in attentions to our Brittish brethren. We have warned them from time to time of attempts by their legislature to extend an unwarrantable jurisdiction over us. We have reminded them of the circumstances of our emigration and settlement here. We have appealed to their native justice and magnanimity, and we have conjured them by the ties of our common kindred to disavow these usurpations, which, would inevitably interrupt our connections and correspondence. They too have been deaf to the voice of justice and of consanguinity. We must, therefore, acquiesce in the necessity, which denounces our Separation, and hold them, as we hold the rest of mankind, Enemies in War, in Peace Friends.

We, therefore, the Representatives of the united States of America, in General Congress, Assembled, appealing to the Supreme Judge of the world for the rectitude of our intentions, do, in the Name, and by Authority of the good People of these Colonies, solemnly publish and declare, That these United Colonies are, and of Right ought to be Free and Independent States; that they are Absolved from all Allegiance to the British Crown, and that all political connection between them and the State of Great Britain, is and ought to be totally dissolved; and that as Free and Independent States, they have full Power to levy War, conclude Peace, contract Alliances, establish Commerce, and to do all other Acts and Things which Independent States may of right do. And for the support of this

Declaration, with a firm reliance on the protection of divine Providence, we mutually pledge to each other our Lives, our Fortunes and our sacred Honor.

The Declaration of Independence came as a result of England's rule that kept the 13 states then constituting America, from living out the original God-given vision as described in the Mayflower Compact, which had been written some 156 years earlier.

THE U.S. CONSTITUTION

It would of course take up too much space to provide you with a copy of the U.S. Constitution and the 27 amendments added to it since it was written. However, reading the Preamble should be enough to convince us that its signers were of the same spirit as those who signed the two former documents:

We the people of the United States, in Order to form a more perfect Union, establish Justice, insure domestic Tranquility, provide for the common defense, promote the general Welfare, and secure the Blessings of Liberty to ourselves and our Posterity, do ordain and establish this Constitution for the United States of America.

An abundance of historical documents is available to anyone who wishes to verify the influence of Christianity on this nation. But for the sake of clarity and the saving of space, I encourage you to read books such as "The 5000 Year Leap" by author W. Cleon Skousen, to get an idea of how much of America's identity was shaped by Christianity and the Holy Scriptures.

Following, is an excerpt from the above-mentioned book, listing 28 great ideas that changed the world and shaped America:

*THE DECLARATION OF INDEPENDENCE – U.S. National Archives & Administration - www.archives.gov

*Note: All historical documents are printed in their original format.

1. *The only reliable basis for sound government and just human relations is natural law.*

2. *A free people cannot survive under a republican constitution unless they remain virtuous and morally strong.*

3. *The most promising method of securing a virtuous and a morally stable people is to elect virtuous leaders.*

4. *Without religion the government of a free people cannot be maintained.*

5. *All things were created by God, therefore upon Him all mankind are equally dependent, and to Him they are equally responsible.*

6. *All men are created equal.*

7. *The proper role of government is to protect inalienable rights of all individuals equally.*

8. *Men are endowed by their creator with certain inalienable rights.*

9. *To protect man's rights, God has revealed certain principles of divine law.*

10. *The God-given right to govern is vested in the sovereign authority of the whole people.*

11. *The people may alter or abolish a government that has become tyrannical.*

12. *The United States shall be a republic.*

13. *A constitution should be structured to permanently protect the people from the human frailties of their rulers.*

14. Life and liberty is secure so long as the right to property is secure.

15. The highest level of prosperity occurs when there is a free market economy and minimum of government regulations.

16. The government should be separated into three branches—legislative, executive and judicial.

17. A system of checks and balances should be adopted to prevent the abuse of power.

18. The unalienable rights of the people are most likely to be preserved if the principles of government are set forth in a written constitution.

19. Only limited and carefully defined powers should be delegated to the government, all others being retained by the people.

20. Efficiency and dispatch require government to operate according to the will of the majority, but constitutional provisions must be made to protect the rights of the minority.

21. Strong local self-government is the keystone to preserving human freedom.

22. A free people should be governed by law and not by the whims of man.

23. A free society cannot survive as a republic without a broad program of general education.

24. A free people will not survive unless they remain strong.

25. Peace, commerce and honest friendship with all nations—entangling alliances with none.

26. The core unit that determines the strength of any society is the family; therefore, the government should foster and protect its integrity.

27. The burden of debt is as destructive to freedom as subjugation by conquest.

28. The United States has a manifest destiny to be an example and a blessing to the entire human race.

For comparison's sake, it is interesting to look at the latest laws implemented by our Progressive politicians and the liberal leaning Supreme Court and see how they stack up against some of these "ideas":

1. **The only reliable basis for sound government and just human relations is natural law.**

Is it any wonder that our current Government seems to act like a drunken sailor? Not only is God's guidance being ignored, but even human logic and practical reason are being cast aside.

2. **A free people cannot survive under a republican constitution unless they remain virtuous and morally strong.**

As morality and virtue are being ridiculed by the media and the majority of American society, we're witnessing the rapid weakening of our great nation.

3. **The most promising method of securing a virtuous and a morally stable people is to elect virtuous leaders.**

How miserably we have failed in this area! While a majority of the American population claims to be Christian, we've elected a known womanizer to two consecutive presidential terms. If that wasn't enough, we twice elected a President who openly embraces Muslim ideology!

WHERE DO WE STAND TODAY?

As I consider how far we have strayed from the original vision, I cannot help but draw a comparison between us as a nation and the Children of Israel. They too escaped the oppression of a nation that didn't share their religious beliefs. The original settlers as well as the signers of the Declaration of Independence, recognized God's special mission for this nation. Their pursuit of liberty wasn't just for the sake of freedom, but it was also for the purpose of bringing a divine vision to pass.

I believe that this divine vision has been neglected, if not completely abandoned.

AMERICA AND THE BIBLE

America's national identity is closely linked to the word of God. The extent to which the Bible inspired the founding documents and shaped the vision of this nation, are undeniable

Ronald Reagan, America's beloved 40th President said:

"Inside the Bible's pages lie all the answers to all of the problems man has ever known. It is my firm belief that the enduring values presented in its pages have a great meaning for each of us and for our nation. The Bible can touch our hearts, order our minds and refresh our souls."

THE GUIDING LIGHT OF THE WORD

Just as Joshua was to follow the guidelines of God's law without wavering, so were the Founding Fathers instructed to use the Bible as a "road map" that would lead them to their desired destination.

Be strong and of good courage, for to this people you shall divide as an inheritance the land which I swore to their fathers to give them. Only be strong and very courageous, that you may observe to do according to all the law which Moses My servant commanded you; do not turn from it to the right hand or to the left, that you may prosper wherever you go. This Book of the Law shall not depart from your mouth, but you shall meditate in it day and night, that you may observe to do according to all that is written in it. For then you will make your way prosperous, and then you will have good success.

Joshua 1:6-8

As a nation, we've obviously deviated from our initial course. But this does not mean that we can't return to the desired "itinerary" God has chosen for us.

*Search from the book of the LORD, and read:
Not one of these shall fail; Not one shall lack her mate.
For My mouth has commanded it, and His Spirit has gathered them. He has cast the lot for them,
And His hand has divided it among them with a measuring line. They shall possess it forever;
From generation to generation they shall dwell in.*

Isaiah 34:16-17

CHAPTER 2

HOW DID WE GET HERE?

My wife and I immigrated to the United States in 1970. Since then, we have witnessed a constant downward progression leading us to where we are today. Most agree that the period following World War II, was one of the most prosperous times in the history of this nation. If we compare the social, financial and military power indicators of that period to today's, we can only come to one conclusion: America is obviously in a perilous "nose dive". The question is: will we be able to recover from it and ultimately reverse it?

There was a time when the citizens of this nation could unashamedly sing: "America, God shed His grace on thee" with great conviction. I believe that this time has now passed and only refers to what used to be.

CONTRIBUTING FACTORS

Being aware of our current situation and reminiscing about days gone by, isn't enough. We must absolutely identify what it is that brought us to where we are today and then decide what we're going to do to change it.

Many factors have contributed to our downfall, but there are some for which, we Christians, share some responsibility: we didn't do enough; write enough letters; engage enough and pray enough to keep this from happening.

As Edmund Burke so famously said:

"The only thing necessary for evil to triumph, is for good men to do nothing".

We have been too complacent, too politically correct and too tolerant toward every religious belief and evil lifestyle, that we've lost our identity and no longer walk in the vision and purpose God called us to. We can continue to sing "America the Beautiful" while hiding our collective heads in the sand, but that won't change the trajectory America has been on. Unless we engage in a concerted effort to take our country back, it will eventually crash and burn.

EVOLVING DEMOGRAPHICS

Immigration in itself is a very good thing, as long as the rules and guidelines are understood, accepted and respected.

The first of these rules applies equally to a household and a hosting country: The guest or would be immigrant, has to either be invited or given permission to enter by the decision-maker of the household or by the recognized authority of the country.

There is a fundamental difference between legal immigration and trespassing. When thousands of people routinely cross the U.S. border without permission or invitation, they shouldn't be treated as immigrants, but rather as trespassers.

As an immigrant and Christian that believes in hospitality, I am perfectly willing to welcome someone into my home, including strangers. In fact, my wife and I have hosted a number of people for a variety of reasons and sometimes for extended periods of time over the years. We never asked for compensation nor did we ever put a lock on the fridge! However, there were certain rules our guests had to abide by.

These were very reasonable and anyone with a minimum of social skills could easily follow them.

For having visited many poor countries during my life in ministry, believe me when I say that I understand why many men and women would want to move to America. But wanting to leave one's native country and desperately wanting to come to another, simply isn't enough.

I can sympathize with the homeless man that wants to get out of the cold, sit in front of the fireplace I just lit and eat the stew my wife has just prepared. But if he breaks into my home to access these things, I can assure you that he won't enjoy them for very long! I can't help but wonder why it's so difficult for some people to understand the meaning of the word "illegal".

The primary purpose for immigration laws, is to monitor the flow of people coming into a nation. They are used to control the provenance, the number and obviously the motives of those wanting to enter the country.

Had a German battalion attempted to cross the Canadian border into the United States in 1943, they certainly would have been met with strong opposition. Why? Because their motives, their provenance and their number represented a threat to this nation.

Today, because we fail to enforce the immigration laws in place and because our borders are so porous, large numbers of people with questionable motives enter this nation illegally every day.

In the past, the influx of immigrants was meticulously controlled. Quotas were established to regulate the number of visas delivered annually to applicants from the Northern and Southern hemispheres. But because illegal immigration is largely tolerated and at times even encouraged, a disproportionate number of people from South America, Central America and Mexico, are coming into our country unrestricted.

Does that pose a problem? It most certainly does! When any group of people from a particular culture or ethnic background, regardless of their origins, grows to the point where it's capable of exercising political pressure on a host country, it represents a real and present danger.

I could give you a number of examples of what I'm talking about. I will only mention one. If you follow the U.S. presidential elections campaign, you will notice that the Latino vote represents such a huge percentage of the population, that no candidate can realistically hope to be elected, unless he or she secures a large segment of that electorate. Historically, Latinos have voted for candidates and programs that are favorable to them and they shouldn't be condemned for this. However, by allowing a disproportionate number of them to enter the country, we've created a huge problem that will only get worse as time goes on.

As bad as this immigration issue is, there's one that is much worse developing as I'm writing this book. There's a plan to welcome between 10,000 and 100,000 Syrian refugees into this country during the next few months. Mind you, these are not Christians fleeing their native country to save their lives. The great majority of them are Muslim men. To be sure, some are fleeing persecution from extremists, but others are simply terrorists taking advantage of an opportunity to enter our country while the doors are wide open.

Allowing large numbers of immigrants from any region of the world to move to a given country can be detrimental. But the problem is further compounded, when the populations we're bringing in have a propensity for organizing politically and tend to promote their ethnicity, rather than the collective good of the host country.

AMERICA'S VISION

Whether we use the word "vision" or not, every company, church or country has a plan or objectives that it follows to achieve a desired result. In the case of America, that vision was given by God to a small group of people, which eventually grew into the greatest nation in the world!

Where there is no vision, the people perish: but he that keepeth the law, happy is he.

Proverbs 29:18   KJV

Just as important as finding a train's destination before boarding it, everyone that is to participate in the American adventure, should be aware of its mission and vision. Without a clear understanding of what our collective target is, people are left to their own misguided and selfish devices.

Our forefathers knew that the land they had just stepped on to, was not just a piece of real estate they were supposed to occupy. They understood what many now ignore and degrade, American exceptionalism.

Benjamin Harrison, America's 23rd President said this about immigration in his Inaugural address:

"Our naturalization laws should be so amended as to make the inquiry into the character and good disposition of persons applying for citizenship more careful and searching. Our existing laws have been in their administration an unimpressive and often an unintelligible form. We accept the man as a citizen without any knowledge of his fitness, and he assumes the duties of

citizenship without any knowledge as to what they are. The privileges of American citizenship are so great and its duties so grave that we may well insist upon a good knowledge of every person applying for citizenship and a good knowledge by him of our institutions. We should not cease to be hospitable to immigration, but we should cease to be careless as to the character of it. There are men of all races, even the best, whose coming is necessarily a burden upon our public revenues or a threat to social order. These should be identified and excluded."

So much for today's unchecked immigration!

AMERICAN EXCEPTIONALISM

In a sense, every nation or people group in the world is exceptional in its own right. France, the country I was born in, has some particularities that distinguishes it from other countries. Whether we understand them or not, we should respect the right of every country to practice and celebrate the things that make them special.

There are certain things that make America special and unique. These are things that define America. To ignore, ridicule or change these particular attributes, is a serious threat to the identity and very fabric of this nation.

July 14th is Bastille Day in France. This commemorates the day when the people of France revolted against the monarchy in 1789. But, since I'm no longer a citizen of France, you will not see a French flag flying from my flagpole, nor will I launch fireworks on my property to commemorate that day. Why? Because I'm an American now. As such, I will celebrate the 4th of July, because America is the country I belong to now!

I don't allow too many things to offend me, but if you really insist on upsetting me, tell me all about the Cinco de Mayo celebration you had with your Mexican friends in Los Angeles last week. If you've become an American citizen, you're no longer Mexican. Didn't you get the memo?

While we're talking about things that upset me, if you're black, please don't introduce yourself as "African American" to me. I am not a "French American", nor are you African. Like me, you're an American with a slightly deeper tan. But I will eventually get over being jealous about it.

OLD THINGS MUST PASS AWAY

There are many similarities between becoming a Christian and becoming a citizen of a new country. We're embracing a new lifestyle, culture and language. In both cases, as one is about to adopt a new citizenship, his allegiances and cultural references must - or at least should be – reassessed.

Therefore, if anyone is in Christ, he is a new creation; old things have passed away; behold, all things have become new.

2 Corinthians 5:17

As Christians, we easily understand that before the new life we aspire to in Christ is to become effective, we must rearrange our priorities, reassess our former relationships and readjust our life focus. The rich young ruler who so wanted to inherit eternal life was told by Jesus that there were two things he needed to do to be qualified: first, he needed to obey God's commandment and second, he had to let go of his dependency on worldly riches.

Millions of people want to come to America to experience a new life in the proverbial "land of opportunity"? But how many are truly willing to abandon the old things in order to allow all things to become new? What most people fail to realize, is that by holding on to the customs, languages and culture they were supposed to leave behind, they are bringing to this country the very things that potentially caused the demise of the country they left behind!

And do not be conformed to this world, but be transformed by the renewing of your mind, that you may prove what is that good and acceptable and perfect will of God.

Romans 12:2

Again, there are many similarities between immigrating to a country such as America and deciding to follow Christ. Whatever "world" an immigrant formerly functioned in, it is required of him to stop conforming to it any longer. He's further asked to renew his way of thinking so as to "prove" that his integration has been successful.

Though it happened some forty years ago, my wife and I distinctly remember being asked to renounce our prior French citizenship. It was explained to us that we had to do this before we could recite the pledge of allegiance and consequently be granted the U.S. citizenship we were seeking.

There are millions of people living in America today that have no intention of giving up their former allegiances, their culture, their lifestyle, their native language or their ideologies.

Am I saying that I should give up my wife's wonderful French cooking or refuse to listen to some of the popular music I grew up on? Not at all!

There are areas in this country, where it's a challenge to find a clerk that understands English just to purchase a souvenir at a store or a waiter from whom to order food at a restaurant. Forgive me! But weren't these people told they were coming to live and work in an English-speaking country?

As Bible-believing Christians, we understand how important a unique language is for a group of people who want to achieve a common goal. Need I remind you that God had to confuse the language of the people of Babel. What was uniting them wasn't just a common goal, but also a common language. This can be found in Genesis 11:9.

Cultural diversity is absolutely wonderful and I actually love to hear different languages being spoken when I travel to other countries. But when people refuse to learn the language that is spoken in the country they choose to become a part of, I can only interpret this to mean that they're not ready to embrace the laws, customs and practices of that country. In that case, they may want to consider the possibility of returning to their native country.

I'm sure that those who are pushing for classes to be taught to immigrant children in their native tongue are well meaning people. But based on my own personal experience, I believe that they're doing these children a great disservice. They're in fact marginalizing these children and hampering their integration into American society.

A COUNTRY DIVIDED

From the time the first pilgrims stepped off the Mayflower and set foot on this great land we call America, it was readily accepted that all those who would later come and join them, would slowly but surely blend in with the already established population.

But this was at a time when our government was by the people and for the people. Everything was done was for the common good and for the advancement of the nation. Today's progressive politicians, will do everything in their power to keep integration from happening. In order to control, manipulate and politically steer the largest individual ethnic groups, they exploit every event and situation for their political advantage. This strategy is one of the oldest in the military handbook. It's called divide and conquer.

"Every kingdom divided against itself is brought to desolation, and every city or house divided against itself will not stand."

Matthew 12:25

THE "BLACK LIVES MATTER" MOVEMENT

One example of the use of this tactic is the riots that are currently being held in major cities around the country. What is being protested is the killing of blacks by police officers. Never mind the fact that those that were killed were often armed, had committed crimes and were resisting arrest. The objection is that these men were black and thus makes it a race crime!

There is neither Jew nor Greek, there is neither slave nor free, there is neither male nor female; for you are all one in Christ Jesus.

Galatians 3:28-29

BATTLEGROUND AMERICA: UNIVERSITY CAMPUSES

After the destructive riots in Ferguson and Baltimore, over totally unjustified complaints against police, black student groups saw an opportunity to take over the University of Missouri. Their protests were over what they perceived to be an unwillingness to act against acts of racism on campus. They succeeded in obtaining the resignation of the University of Missouri system President, Tim Wolfe. Outside of knowing a few students that attend the school, I don't know much about the University of Missouri, but I have serious doubts about the charges of racism directed at a school that elected a black student as their campus president.

Not only do I believe that black lives matter, but they're very precious to God. I also believe that Asian lives, native American, Latino and white lives matter just as much. Listening to the arguments of the movement' leaders, I get the uneasy impression that what they're defending is the notion that black lives are actually more valuable than anyone else's.

It is very unfortunate and dangerous that the current resident of the White House would support the "Black Lives Matter" movement. Just as he obliviously cares more about Islamic extremists than the victims of their atrocities, he defends the cause of agitators, criminals and vandals, more than the police force that tries to protect us from them. He is in the process of erasing all the wonderful progress made in the area of civil rights over the past 50 years!

Again, black lives very much matter. I just wish agitators such as Al Sharpton would draw the black community's attention to organizations such as Planned Parenthood, who's founder, Margaret Sanger, was a notorious racist. Following is a quote from an article she wrote on page 108 of the Birth Control Review in April of 1932:

"Birth control must lead ultimately to a cleaner race"

Before moving on to another subject, I'd like to know what the definition of "African American" is. Should I begin to identify myself as a "French American"? I was born in another country, but I am now proud to be an American.

In 2008, when Michelle Obama declared that for the first time in her life she was proud of America, was she saying that she had no reason to be proud of this country until that point? After almost 8 years of "change" so generously provided by her husband, I believe that many of the reasons that made us proud to be Americans, have dissipated. When I travel to other countries of the world today, I no longer volunteer that I'm an American. I just became tired of the look of disdain I was receiving every time I did.

Instead of looking in the same direction and working together to accomplish the purpose God has called us to as a nation, we've allowed politicians, much more concerned about their careers than the advancement of America, to manipulate us and divide us.

By the way, should anyone get the false idea that I have a racial bias, they're welcome to check how much humanitarian relief my wife and I have provided to African populations over the years and put that thought to rest.

CHAPTER 3

THE STORY OF TWO IMMIGRANTS

For anyone who was born and raised in America, it might be difficult to understand why so many people would put forth such tremendous effort and in some cases, face tremendous danger to immigrate to the United States.

I'm sure there are multiple valid reasons. As for my wife and I, we'd progressively lost all trust in the increasingly Socialist French government and couldn't see our way clear to a decent future, had we decided to remain there.

At the time that we made our decision to immigrate, I was working for the French Railroad. Since it was a nationalized enterprise, I was receiving all the benefits of a government agent. I had the benefits of full medical coverage, free train transportation, guaranteed pension and was assured absolute job security.

I still remember the conversations my wife and I had about our future in France: if all went well, I could someday become the manager of a small town railroad station. This career goal was so utopist at the time, that we could hardly imagine the possibilities. For reference, my first paycheck from Ford Motor Company, where I first worked after coming to America, was substantially higher than that of a manager of a small French railroad station!

This may sound silly to you, but while in France, we longingly looked forward to the day when we'd have our own telephone! A week after moving to the States, we proudly watched, as our first telephone was installed in our apartment.

FINDING THE LAND OF OPPORTUNITY

When someone comes to America, the first thing he notices, are the limitless opportunities open to him. In spite of the challenges of learning a new language and adapting to a different culture, it quickly became obvious to me that there were business opportunities all around me, just waiting to be embraced. Within a few months of working at the auto plant, I was running a side business that produced enough income to pay for my family's annual cross country vacations.

Even in today's economy, I refuse to accept the notion that jobs are hard to find in America. One might find it difficult to find employment in his field of experience, but if one has enough self-esteem to support himself and his family and refuse handouts, he will do whatever it takes to earn a decent living.

The problem we currently have is that we've taught an entire generation that they're entitled to an income, whether they've earned it or not. In some neighborhoods, young people seeking employment, are actually ridiculed by their peers because it "isn't cool" to work, when you can make so much more money drawing government benefits while selling crack cocaine on the street!

I am absolutely convinced that business and job opportunities are still plentiful in America today. What we're increasingly lacking, are men and women willing to do whatever work needs to be done!

"The harvest truly is plentiful, but the laborers are few. Therefore, pray the Lord of the harvest to send out laborers into His harvest."

Matthew 9:37-38

BORN IN AMERICA

When someone decides to come to the States and actually wants to do it legally, it can be a lengthy and complicated process. Because we had been granted a special status due to the mother/daughter relationship of my wife to an American citizen, we had not anticipated that it would take as long as it did to obtain our visa. My wife was pregnant with our second child, Delphine. I must point out that Delphine was in no way being used as an "anchor baby" in order to get into the United States. Thank God, Josette showed very little evidence of pregnancy until the final weeks. As the formalities dragged on, we began to fear that the airline company would refuse to let my wife onto the plane.

Josette had entered the seventh month of pregnancy, when we made what would be our last trip to the American Embassy in Paris. We presented our case as we had done many times before, receiving pretty much the same response: "we're processing your request and you just need to be patient. We will contact you as soon as you're accepted."

Perhaps out of desperation or maybe inspiration, my wife cried out: "I want my child to be born in America"! This plea must have struck a chord in the heart of the immigration agent on duty, because from that moment on, things moved rather quickly and we obtained our visa within just a few weeks.

HUMBLE BEGINNINGS

The first employment I held when my family and I came to America, was an assembly line job at an auto plant.

Did I like it? Not one bit! Did I want to finish my life building cars only other people would end up driving? Certainly not! But I was happy, nevertheless, about having a good paying job, along with health insurance and other benefits.

From the moment I walked out of the human resources office of the Wayne Assembly plant and started working at my assigned position, I knew that this was not what I had come to America for. At that moment, I made the conscious decision to decline this job, for which I was extremely grateful, as a fatality. It wasn't that I felt that this kind of work was beneath me, but I was keenly aware of the limitless opportunities that offered themselves to me.

While I continued to work on the assembly line, I began to sell my own artwork to the other employees. I also sold the beverage containers that my wife would deliver to me during break time. Did we get rich by doing this? Not according to worldly economic standards. But it allowed us to enjoy a lifestyle that was measurably better than that of a factory worker and way beyond the one we would have had we stayed in France.

THINGS GET PROGRESSIVELY BETTER

My wife, our three children and I, subsequently moved to Colorado, to start a business. To say that our first business venture was a failure, would be an understatement! But that didn't keep us from trying… By the time we entered the ministry in 1987, we had run a number of various enterprises, for the most part successful.

You probably never had to deal with the red tape and tremendous obstacles one has to overcome in an environment such as France, but believe me when I say that the opportunities to succeed in America were tremendous by comparison.

MEETING JESUS IN AMERICA

One Spring morning in 1972, I asked Jesus to come into my heart. I was sitting in a restaurant parking lot across from the plant I had been working at since first moving to America. You may ask: "what does this have to do with what's happening in America today?" I believe it has everything to do with it! Had the spiritual condition been what it is today, I seriously doubt that anybody would have presented me the plan of salvation in such an open and sincere fashion.

At the time that my wife and I came to this country, America was very much a Christian nation, regardless of what some might say. Before coming here, we had spent more than 20 years of our lives without ever having the love of Jesus presented to us.

Christianity has become marginalized and political correctness increasingly dictates what we can and cannot do in this nation, making it increasingly more difficult to share the love of Christ with people outside of the church environment.

WHAT DO YOU LOVE ABOUT AMERICA?

During the 46 plus years my wife and I have been in the United States, we've often been asked what it is that attracted us to America and, most importantly, what kept us here.

Quite honestly, our motivation for coming to this country initially, was more about leaving France, than it was about choosing America. We didn't know enough about this nation to make that choice. We only knew that we couldn't continue to live in the socialistic environment we grew up in.

Progressively, our eyes were opened to all the possibilities that were offered to us. We slowly discovered the land of liberty and opportunity that America truly was.

It might help you understand why I'm so determined to fight for this nation to keep it from becoming what my family and I escaped from.

THE BROKEN PROMISE OF SOCIALISM

To help you understand the devastating effects of socialism in Europe, I feel it is necessary to give you a snapshot of what the environment is like in most countries of the E.U. Because an increasingly growing portion of the population is benefiting from the entitlements that have thus far been generously showered upon them, few attempts have been made to reverse them. Here are just a few examples:

- French workers have a 35 hour work week. Any work time beyond that, has to be treated as overtime.

  Just in case you find yourself envying your French counterparts, or even secretly wishing this would happen here in America, put yourself in the shoes of the business owner that has to maintain high production levels under these conditions.

  I have a longtime personal friend in France that was exactly in that position. He had taken over his family's business, which consisted of the manufacturing of industrial wheels of every size and variety. When the 35 hour work week was implemented, it became almost impossible to keep the operation profitable. Since the Lord had already called my friend to the pastoral ministry, he decided to sell the company...if he could. He eventually sold the factory to a German conglomerate, which was nothing short of a miracle!

- Anyone that's been employed for more than a year, is entitled to 5 weeks paid vacation annually. Imagine what this does to company's bottom line! No wonder so many European enterprises are relocating to other countries, where it's still possible to run a business.

- Besides a 5 week vacation, every employee is allowed up to 4 weeks worth of sick days per year, for which he or she is fully paid!

Not only is the employer financially responsible for this, but he is also required to match whatever he pays his employees with an equal amount to be paid out to the government!

Before you cast your vote for anyone that promises to bring this so-called "paradise" to our country, you might want to factor in our national debt of 19 trillion and climbing, and consider the number of companies that would most certainly relocate to more fiscally favorable countries.

Margaret Thatcher, the former Prime Minister of Great Britain said this about Socialism:

"Socialism is a wonderful thing... Until you run out of somebody else's money!"

What she described is exactly what began to happen in France. For many years, successive French Socialist governments played Robin Hood with other people's hard earned money.

Factory after factory began to close. Long-established companies found it impossible to do business in this kind of environment and were forced to leave the country. When government leaders began to see the writing on the wall and realize that they would soon run out of other people's money, they had to come up with a solution.

Without the possibility of continuing on the same course, they, and a number of other European leaders found themselves in what in football is called a punting situation. But who could they kick this unmanageable football to? Aha! They would form an economic coalition of nations, which would buy them the time they needed, until they could come up with a more permanent solution. And thus, the European Union was birthed.

I believe that from the inception, the promoters of the European Union concept knew that this would only be a temporary fix. But they thought that it could be a perfect stepping stone to prepare the world for what they see as the ultimate solution: Globalization and a One World Government.

Greece, Portugal, Italy, and France are increasingly facing deep financial problems. The recent massive migration of refugees from the Middle East has complicated Europe's economic problems even further. Germany has thus far been carrying most of the financial burden. But this too, will eventually come to an end!

When the day finally comes, and the E.U. finds itself in yet another "punting" situation", to whom will it kick the ball? Let me guess… the answer seems obvious. The Antichrist will only be too happy to offer his services and deceive the masses into believing that he alone can bring a permanent solution to the world's problems.

Unless you've been keeping up with world affairs, you may find it difficult to agree with my conclusions. But time will tell whether I'm right or not. Bible prophecy seems to agree with the scenario I just presented. But I'll let you be the judge.

CHAPTER 4

AMERICA'S MORAL DECLINE

"When you become entitled to exercise the right of voting for public officers, let it be impressed on your mind that God commands you to choose for rulers, "just men who will rule in the fear of God." The preservation of [our] government depends on the faithful discharge of this Duty; if the citizens neglect their Duty and place unprincipled men in office, the government will soon be corrupted; laws will be made, not for the public good so much as for selfish or local purposes; corrupt or incompetent men will be appointed to execute the Laws; the public revenues will be squandered on unworthy men; and the rights of the citizen will be violated or disregarded. If [our] government fails to secure public prosperity and happiness, it must be because the citizens neglect the Divine Commands, and elect bad men to make and administer the Laws."

History of the United States by Noah Webster.

It would be very difficult to pinpoint the exact time when America began its downward spiral. But we can identify three major historical events that contributed to it in a major way:

- The 1963 Supreme Court decision in the Murray vs. Curlett case which banned prayer in Public Schools.

.*THEHISTORY OF AMERICA – By Noah Webster
https://www.noahwebsterhouse.org/.../noah-webster-history.htm

- The Viet Nam anti-war protests
- The 1973 Roe vs. Wade Supreme Court ruling on legalizing abortion.

THE BANNING OF PRAYER IN PUBLIC SCHOOLS

This was a significant event, not only because it forbade Christian expression from the educational process of our children, but it set in motion a trend that led to the banning of Bible reading in schools and eventually to the exclusion of Christian symbols and the mention of God in public settings.

Today, hardly a month goes by, without a report of someone being challenged for praying or expressing gratitude to the Lord during sporting events, school activities or military celebrations.

THE VIET NAM ANTI-WAR PROTESTS

What most people remember about the late 60's, are the popular songs of that era and the iconic "No to the Bomb" emblem that defined this entire generation.

Most of us don't realize how much of an impact that cultural revolution really had on this nation.

I wasn't living in the United States at the time, but France was experiencing a similar societal shift during the same period. Students were rioting in the streets of Paris, in opposition to what they felt was society's infringement of their civil liberties. The slogan of the revolt was: "Il est interdit d'interdire", meaning "it is forbidden to forbid"!

So significant was this movement, that it gave birth to a brand new way of thinking. Unlike the authors of the French revolution of 1789, the people that embraced this new culture weren't just rebelling against a particular form of government. They were anarchists in the purest sense of the word, refusing to submit to the laws of men and of God.

Let every soul be subject to the governing authorities. For there is no authority except from God, and the authorities that exist are appointed by God.

Romans 13:1

The events of 1968 in France brought about a completely new way of thinking in France. Riots, demonstrations, acts of vandalism and massive labor strikes, became a national pastime! Hardly a month went by without a major strike paralyzing the nation. Teachers unions, transportation syndicates and other industries actually coordinated the scheduling of their strikes to maximize the negative impact they'll have on the population. On a humoristic note, this practice had become so accepted, that the Parisian prostitutes once organized a strike to be granted more social benefits and greater respect for their "profession"!

When it comes to vandalism, it can be found absolutely everywhere in France! It is practically impossible to find a square inch of wall, bridge, fence or railroad car in Paris, that's not been marred by tagging. But it goes much further than that! Every time a minority group feels they've been victimized, they routinely set automobiles on fire, vandalize storefronts and destroy private and public property. These practices have become so accepted by French society, that the police no longer get involved and rarely are arrests ever made.

We could easily be fooled into thinking that such things could never happen here in the United States. Really? What do you think recently happened in Ferguson, Baltimore and St Louis?

THE BLOOD OF THE INNOCENT

Since the Roe vs. Wade ruling by the Supreme Court of the United States on abortion in 1973, we've killed millions of innocent babies. We have collectively murdered these children in direct violation of God's law and the will of America's Founding Fathers. Do we really believe that this won't have an adverse effect on this nation?

In the first pages of the American Patriot's Bible, Dr. Richard Lee lists the "Dignity of Human Life" as the first principle of Judeo Christian ethics:

The Scriptures emphatically teach the great importance of the respect and preservation of human life. In the Declaration of Independence, our nation's Founding Fathers wrote that every man, woman and child has the right to "life, liberty and the pursuit of happiness." We Americans not only believe this for our land, but we also send our brave men and women in our military forces across the world to defend the rights of those whose lives are threatened.

If people and nations do not grant this respect and protection for the born and unborn, all other professed morals and values are meaningless, because they are no longer undergirded by the most basic of human needs—the need to exist. The dignity of human life is not just a principle of the Bible—it is the beginning principle of any civilized society.

THE GAY MARRIAGE ISSUE

When it come to events that have contributed to the decline of America, it is impossible to ignore the significance of the recent ruling by the United States Supreme Court on gay marriage.

This could be perceived as just another item to be checked off the liberal agenda, but it goes much deeper than that.

To be sure, homosexual practices have been around for a very long time. But until recent years, the gay lifestyle was perceived as unusual and shameful. Today, it is considered to be normal and even somewhat fashionable. Major U.S. companies are spending millions of dollars in advertizing money to reach the gay population of this country.

I previously quoted Dr. Richard G. Lee when I wrote about abortion in America. I would like to reference what he wrote about the traditional monogamous family in his "Principles of Judeo-Christian Ethics":

"The biblical view of marriage and family is the basis of our society and serves as the backbone of a healthy social order. The clear plan of God involves a man and a woman producing children within the institution of marriage. Since the joining together of Adam and Eve, marriage has been defined as a holy union between one man and one woman, and out of that union comes children born into a loving home with a father and a mother to nurture them and teach them how to become healthy, productive and responsible citizens. When God's definition of "marriage" and "family" are no longer respected, these institutions become meaningless. World history has proven over and again that preserving the traditional family is vital to the future of any great nation."

The ancient cities of Sodom and Gomorrah had a long-standing reputation of being wicked. They certainly didn't wait for Lot to move in to town, to begin their evil lifestyle.

But the men of Sodom were exceedingly wicked and sinful against the LORD.

Genesis 13:13

We know from scriptures, that there were less than ten righteous in the entire city of Sodom. We also know that both the young and the old were equally guilty of this wickedness.

What we don't know, is how long this went on before God decided to bring judgment on these two cities. I wonder how much the words Lot spoke to the men of Sodom, precipitated the course of events:

Now before they lay down, the men of the city, the men of Sodom, both old and young, all the people from every quarter, surrounded the house. And they called to Lot and said to him, "Where are the men who came to you tonight? Bring them out to us that we may know them carnally." So Lot went out to them through the doorway, shut the door behind him, and said, "Please, my brethren, do not do so wickedly!

Genesis 19:4-7

"My brethren"? We don't know when Lot began to identify at that level with these corrupt individuals and their wicked practices. What is certain, is that he could have addressed them in many different ways: heathen, vile men, perverts. However, he made the unfortunate choice of calling them "Brethren"!

Until Jesus returns to reign in the affairs of men, there is no indication that evil practices will cease or even be curbed. On the contrary, we're warned that things will get progressively worse.

But that doesn't mean that we should accept this progression of evil, as an inevitable fatality. No matter how bad our earthly environment becomes, it does not exempt us from exercising our God-given spiritual authority or forfeit our responsibility of being salt and light on this earth.

Besides the approval of gay marriage, there are many other ways our current administration is catering to the LGBT agenda. Our military is forbidden to wear their uniforms to participate in a Christian event. On the other hand, it is perfectly O.K. for them to wear it during a gay parade!

You shall not lie with a male as with a woman. It is an abomination.

Leviticus 18:22

What disturbs me the most about this issue, is how many pastors are willing to discard the word of God, to accommodate the gay community. As much as we are to love men and women who struggle with their sexuality, we cannot accept it, sanction it or embrace it, and certainly shouldn't marry them. Which part of this sin God calls an abomination don't these preachers understand?

HUMANISM IN AMERICA

The influence of humanism on American society has been a slow and gradual process and its effects are increasingly being felt.

We must understand that humanism perceives God as a competitor in the race for the control of mankind. Our universities and public schools today are educating our young men and women in the ways of humanism. Whether they admit it or not, most countries of Europe have adopted humanism as their unofficial religion. America is quickly catching up.

If you doubt the influence of humanism on American society, just look at the 2008 and 2012 presidential elections. How do you explain the percentage of voters that twice supported a humanist candidate, in spite of his views on abortion, gay rights and anti-Christian rhetoric.

WHAT JUST HAPPENED?

Societal changes don't generally happen overnight. Any force able to apply consistent pressure in a certain direction, will eventually alter the course of whatever that force is applied to.

For many years, America was on a blessed course that caused the admiration or the jealousy of many nations of the world. It seemed that there was no limit to what this country could achieve.

One might wonder what happened. Paul had similar questions concerning the Galatian Church, which also had the potential of achieving great things for the Lord. Apparently, someone influenced them, causing them to alter their course which almost resulted in them forfeiting their godly destiny.

You ran well. Who hindered you from obeying the truth?
This persuasion does not come from Him who calls you. A
little leaven leavens the whole lump.

Galatians 5:7-10

One of the most insidious forces that's been applied on American society, is the negative influence of our education system. Stopping prayer in school is only the first step that paved the way for what is happening today. The American school system has been high jacked by ultra-liberal teachers, who are using the classroom as platforms to influence and shape the minds of young students.

Instead of teaching our young men and women the principles and values that made this country great, the vast majority of teachers are indoctrinating our children in ways that would cause the founding fathers to turn over in their graves!

I thought it was appropriate to quote excerpts from the Current Communist Goals from the "Naked Communist" book by Cleon Skousen, as communicated to the US House of Representatives on January 10, 1963.

Get control of the schools. Use them as transmission belts for socialism and current Communist propaganda. Soften the curriculum. Get control of teacher's associations. Put the party line in textbooks."

Gain control of all student newspapers.

Use student riots to foment public protests against programs or organizations which are under Communist attack.

Eliminate prayer or any phase of religious expression in the schools on the ground that it violates the principle of "separation of church and state".

Present homosexuality, degeneracy and promiscuity as "normal, natural and healthy".

Discredit the American Constitution by calling it inadequate, old-fashioned, out of step with modern needs,

a hindrance to cooperation between nations on a worldwide basis.

Discredit the American Founding Fathers. Present them as selfish aristocrats who had no concern for the "common man".

Belittle all forms of American culture and discourage the teaching of American history on the ground that it was only a minor part of the "big picture". Give more emphasis to Russian history since the communists took over.

Support any socialist movement to give centralized control over any part of the culture-education, social agencies, welfare programs, mental health clinics, etc.

This last one has nothing to do with the American education system, but I thought it necessary to include, in light of what's been happening in Ferguson, Baltimore and other U.S. cities:

Transfer some of the powers of arrest from the police to social agencies. Treat all behavioral problems as psychiatric disorders which no one but psychiatrists can understand (or treat)."

Hard to believe that this was read in the U.S. House of Representatives over 56 years ago!

LOOK WHAT THEY'VE DONE TO MY SONG

I already explained the reasons for which my wife and I decided to leave France some 46 years ago. What I didn't say, is how the horrific environment we found ourselves in, came about.

Shortly after WW II, communist propaganda began to infiltrate the media and higher education in France. This influence began to shape the collective mindset of the population in such a way that it pinned the less affluent people, against those that had greater financial means.

People with money, business owners and factory directors, were painted as the enemy of the rest of the population. Riots against employers multiplied and debilitating strikes eventually became France's national pastime. Every fall, at the time when most businesses were trying to recover from the effects of the summer slowdown, it had become somewhat of a tradition for teachers and public transportation employees to take turns going on strike. While the effects of these strikes were painful to the general population of major cities, the negative impact on the businesses was catastrophic!

To help you understand how insane things have become, allow me to relate a personal experience I had during one of my many visits to my native country:

The incident took place in the city of Grenoble, a beautiful city at the foot of the French Alps. The employees of a local company were on strike to demand higher wages and better working conditions. I don't know if their demands were legitimate or not, but the way they went about it proved to me how unreasonable humans without God can become! Here they were, driving through the center of town, on their bosses' time, in their company's vehicles, using gas the company had provided!

It gets worse! Several years ago, right before the Christmas celebrations, groups of unemployed people decided to loot French grocery stores, delicatessens and liquor stores of major cities. They claimed that it was unfair for them to not receive a year-end bonus, just because they weren't working. Believe it or not, their cause was heard and they received their bonus, all at tax payers expense!

CHAPTER 5

WHAT'S GOING ON?

Let me begin this chapter by saying that until Jesus finally rules the world during the millennium, there won't be a perfect government on the earth.

It is better to trust in the LORD
Than to put confidence in man.
It is better to trust in the LORD
Than to put confidence in princes.

Psalms 118:8-9

The degree of submission of government leaders to divine guidance and to the guidelines of His word, determines the ultimate success of a nation. America has certainly had its ups and downs, but never has there been such disregard for God and the Judeo-Christian principles this country was built on.

Our Founding Fathers perfectly understood this reality. Please read this excerpt from the Rhode Island Charter of 1683:

"We submit our persons, lives and estates unto our Lord Jesus Christ, the King of Kings, and Lord of Lords, to all those perfect and most absolute laws of His given to us in His Holy Word."

*Note: All historical documents are printed in their original format.

THE AMERICAN "VERSAILLES"

In the middle of the 17th century, King Louis the 14th, nicknamed the "Sun King" started the building of the palace of Versailles.

The king and his court had lived comfortably in the sumptuous buildings that house the Louvres Museum today. You would think that at 652,298 square feet, the king's residence in Paris should have been sufficient. Lack of space, however, was not the reason for relocation. What Louis the 14th wanted, was a place where he could organize and better control the government of France and freely impose absolute personal rule.

We have a de facto "royal palace" called the White House in America today. Within the Washington D.C. beltway, you find a modern day "Versailles" that is totally disconnected from the rest of the country.

When "king" Obama surveys his privileged environment, he comes away with the illusion that all is well in America.

At a time when the people were suffering from severe hunger all across France, the wife of Louis the 16th, another Versailles royal occupant, responded to the population's request by saying: "If they don't have bread, let them eat cake!"

Just like our President today, she was totally out of touch with reality. Subsequently, she lost her head at the beginning of the French revolution.

The similar mindsets of these leaders are astounding. May America undergo such a spiritual revolution so as to reverse the catastrophic effects of having arrogant and control hungry rulers lead our nation any longer.

GOD'S CHOICE: GOD-FEARING RULERS

In order for His chosen people to enjoy freedom and be given an opportunity to pursue happiness, God instituted a form of government in Israel that insured His continuous input and allowed for His sovereign will to be implemented.

And when the LORD raised up judges for them, the LORD was with the judge and delivered them out of the hand of their enemies all the days of the judge; for the LORD was moved to pity by their groaning because of those who oppressed them and harassed them.

Judges 2:18

To this end, He gave them judges that were first, accountable to Him and second, called to serve God's people. Although not officially, Moses and Joshua actually functioned as de facto judges. The principle behind this form of government is that it functioned on the basis of delegated authority. The judge could only exercise this authority over the people within the boundaries of God's directives to His people.

And it came to pass, when the judge was dead, that they reverted and behaved more corruptly than their fathers, by following other gods, to serve them and bow down to them. They did not cease from their own doings nor from their stubborn way.

Judges 2:19

Here again, even this form of government proved to have its weaknesses. Let's face it, as long as a government has to rely on humans, it is eventually bound to fail.

ISRAEL WANTS A KING

Just like most of Americans today, Israel didn't want God to interfere with their lives. They eventually asked to be given a king.

"Now make us a king to judge us like all the nations."

1 Samuel 8:5

The people apparently felt cheated for not having a king "like all the nations." They desperately wanted a change in the way they were governed. Samuel warned them that the "change" they were asking for, wasn't going to be as great as they anticipated. I wish more people had paid attention when several preachers, myself included, warned about the changes then presidential candidate Barak Hussein Obama would bring to this nation!

"This will be the behavior of the king who will reign over you: He will take your sons and appoint them for his own chariots and to be his horsemen, and some will run before his chariots. He will appoint captains over his thousands and captains over his fifties, will set some to plow his ground and reap his harvest, and some to make his weapons of war and equipment for his chariots. He will take your daughters to be perfumers, cooks, and bakers. And he will take the best of your fields, your vineyards, and your

olive groves, and give them to his servants. He will take a tenth of your grain and your vintage, and give it to his officers and servants. And he will take your male servants, your female servants, your finest young men, and your donkeys, and put them to his work. He will take a tenth of your sheep. And you will be his servants. And you will cry out in that day because of your king whom you have chosen for yourselves, and the LORD will not hear you in that day."

1 Samuel 8:11-18

If there's one thing that President Obama will be remembered for is that he did his best to bring America down to the level of every other nation of the world. You might remember some of the early presidential visits to foreign countries, when our president actually apologized for America's so called arrogance. What does he perceive as arrogance? It's the fact that America is different from every other country in the world. To this president, the things that make this nation exceptional, are an embarrassment.

FOLLOWING IN EUROPE'S FOOTSTEPS

The effort to dilute the sovereignty of individual nations and willingly diminish the power of a nation is nothing new.

I know that what I'm about to say will very much sound like a conspiracy theory, but I am deeply convinced that the current occupant of the White House is deliberately doing everything in his power to bring this country down, in preparation for a one world government.

CONSTITUTIONAL REPUBLIC vs DEMOCRACY

While America has spent much money, spilled many soldiers blood and diplomatically worked at helping other nations in implementing democratic law, we have lost sight of the fact that we're not a democracy, but rather a Constitutional Republic.

America's Founding Fathers understood the difference between the two. They understood that only a Constitutional Republic would be able to avoid the extreme of tyranny or mobocracy.

You may not be familiar with the term mobocracy, but it simply means that an organized mob that gathers enough media attention, is able to sway public opinion and the government in a way that benefits them. The recent riots of pro illegal immigration protesters on the streets of America, are a perfect example of mobocracy. Bill S. 2611 was passed by the U.S. Senate without going through the democratic process of consultation with the individual states.

VOTING MATTERS

Many people have become disillusioned and have completely lost trust in the government. I understand their frustration. But this should not result in our complete withdrawal from the political process. If we don't vote because we feel that the "game" is rigged and our participation meaningless, we surrender to the very enemies of our country and forgo the right to complain if things get worse in our nation, and they will!

Pardon me if I seem a bit redundant by repeating the following quote from Edmund Burke:

"The only thing necessary for the triumph of evil is for good men to do nothing."

Fellow Christian, please hear me when I say: "it does matter who you vote for". If you voted for a pro-abortion, pro gay, pro One World Government president in 2008, may God forgive you. But if you re-elected the one I believe to be the forerunner of the antichrist, in 2012, sorry, but allow me to question your Christian ethics.

CHAPTER 6

THE ENEMY WITHIN

It is impossible for a country like America not to have enemies. Some will choose to be against us because of political differences or because we don't share their ideology. We may not understand why there would be such animosity towards a wonderful country such as ours and a people as charming as we are.

If it is possible, as much as depends on you, live peaceably with all men.

Romans 12:18

Andrew Jackson, the 7th President of the United States, had a clear understanding of America's special destiny. One thing that particularly stands out to me in his speech, was his warning that the greatest threat to America's liberty and happiness would not come from abroad, *but "from cupidity, from corruption, from disappointed ambition and inordinate thirst for power."*

What insight! In light of what's currently happening in our nation, this warning couldn't have been more prophetically accurate!

We obviously shouldn't go out of our way to antagonize people. But we need to recognize that not everyone will be a friend to America.

In the past few years, much has been done to accommodate and make friends with nations that have openly declared themselves to be our enemies and openly desire the death of America. We are actually financing the terrorist efforts and nuclear arms program of one such nation, namely Iran!

If a private citizen of any country was caught being involved in such activities, he would most certainly be prosecuted for treason and punished accordingly.

Our own President is engaging in activities that threaten the very existence of Israel, America and the rest of the world. There's only one thing I can say about this: with friends like this, who needs enemies?

THE PROVERBIAL TROJAN HORSE

The jury is still out on whether the story of the Trojan horse is a historical fact or belongs to Greek mythology. Either way, the strategy called by that name, has proven to be extremely effective over time. When an enemy is allowed to penetrate an otherwise secured place, it is called a Trojan horse.

Because of porous borders and misguided immigration laws, we're allowing thousands of enemies of America to penetrate this land to plan, organize, strategize and train for the purpose of causing harm to the citizens of this nation.

At the writing of this book, hardly a day goes by without some act of terror being committed by people whose intentions were known or should have been known, before they were allowed to enter into the U.S.

A NON- HOSTILE TAKEOVER

Right here in America, we're witnessing the obvious and progressive takeover of one of our cities. Situated in the suburbs of Detroit, Michigan, this locality has been strategically chosen by the Islamic leadership, as an experimental pilot for the future expansion of Muslim occupation in America. Over the years, we've seen one business after another being taken over by Muslims. Property rentals or purchases by non-Muslims are increasingly curtailed in Dearborn.

Recent rumors about the city of Dearborn implementing Sharia law in that community, have proven to be false. But this doesn't mean that all is well in Dearborn! There are many Muslim countries that don't apply Sharia law, including the country of Pakistan, which I recently visited. But ask any Christian living there how they're being treated and they will tell you that they live in constant fear and that they enjoy none of the protection or benefits afforded the Muslim population.

I used to believe that some of our political leaders were incredibly naïve or incurably stupid. I've now concluded that they're neither. They're very much aware of what is taking place in our country, but they're unwilling to do anything about it.

At the time of this writing, there are 35 terrorist training camps operating on U.S. territory. Our government officials are very much aware of their existence and know the nature of the activities within these camps. But under the pretext of freedom of expression, they refuse to take action against them!

TRUTH OR CONSPIRACY THEORY?

I've always been very skeptical of all the conspiracy theories you read about on the internet. It has been increasingly more difficult to distinguish between what is real and what is the product of someone's overactive imagination.

This doesn't mean that we should treat every bit of information we gather with suspicion. Reports have been made that Obama, our current President, was believed to be the Antichrist. Personally, I find that hard to believe. But considering how much this man has done to weaken America's militarily, morally and economically, and the conscious efforts he's made to level the playing field in preparation for a future One World Government, I have no doubt that he is a forerunner for the one that will one day lead the world in the greatest deception that has ever been perpetrated against mankind.

CHAPTER 7

WHAT'S NEXT?

The last thing I want is for this book to discourage you or cause you to give up on America. The nation of Israel disobeyed God, rebelled against Him and followed idols of every kind during the course of history. But that did not result in God's forsaking His chosen people.

Albeit in a different way, there's an unwritten covenant that exists between God and the people of America. At the root of this covenant is America's mandate to protect Israel. Another important element of this covenant is America's calling to send missionaries around the world.

Because I sincerely believe in the reality of this covenant and because I'm certain that it is still in effect, I urge you not to give up on America.

We may never regain our position as the first military or financial power in the world, but I'm not so sure that this was God's goal in the first place. When the U.S. Constitution was signed on September 17, 1787, America was far from being a superpower! But it was rightly positioned to accomplish the mission God had called it to execute. I believe that if men and women in America recognize that this is in fact a time of God's visitation for this nation, we will experience the greatest revival this country has ever seen!

KNOWING THE TIMES

It is absolutely essential that we discern the times that we live in, both individually and as a nation. According to Ecclesiastes, there's a time for every purpose under heaven. I beseech you not to be like the Pharisees of Jesus' time, which had no trouble perceiving things in the natural, but were totally blind when it came to spiritual things.

"You can discern the face of the sky and of the earth, but how

is it you do not discern this time?"

Luke 12:56

Not being able to discern the time we live in, can have severe consequences. Because the people of Jerusalem failed to recognize the time of their visitation, they opened themselves to catastrophic events.

**"If you had known, even you, especially in this your day,
the things that make for your peace! But now they are
hidden from your eyes.   For days will come upon you when
your enemies will build an embankment around you,
surround you and close you in on every side, and level you,
and your children within you, to the ground; and they will
not leave in you one stone upon another, because you did
not know the time of your visitation."**

Luke 19:42-44

The same holds true for us individually as Christians. Queen Esther almost missed her entire life purpose. Had it not been for her Uncle Mordecai's admonition, she would have forfeited her very destiny.

And Mordecai told them to answer Esther: "Do not think in your heart that you will escape in the king's palace any more than all the other Jews. For if you remain completely silent at this time, relief and deliverance will arise for the Jews from another place, but you and your father's house will perish. Yet who knows whether you have come to the kingdom for such a time as this?"

Esther 4:13-14

There are several very important lessons we can learn from this passage of scriptures:

1. **Refusing to stand for God and justice, will not keep us from suffering the effects of an enemy's attack.**

   Case in point: For many years now, European nations have failed to stand against the onslaught of Islamic aggression for fear of reprisals. Today, they're suffering the effects of their passivity.

2. **God's purpose will be accomplished, whether we participate in His plan or if He has to turn to another individual or another nation.**

   When Saul miserably failed as the first king of Israel, God was not left without options. David, who truly had a heart for God, fulfilled His plan in a more glorious way than Saul ever could.

3. **This stresses the importance of knowing what our calling and responsibilities are.**

Instead of complaining about what's happening in the world and more specifically in America, we would be wise to concentrate on what we can do to reverse the trend and see it as an opportunity to engage in what God is doing in the world and in America.

"O Lord, great and awesome God, who keeps His covenant and mercy with those who love Him, and with those who keep His commandments, we have sinned and committed iniquity, we have done wickedly and rebelled, even by departing from Your precepts and Your judgments. Neither have we heeded Your servants the prophets, who spoke in Your name to our kings and our princes, to our fathers and all the people of the land.

O Lord, righteousness belongs to You, but to us shame of face, as it is this day — to the men of Judah, to the inhabitants of Jerusalem and all Israel, those near and those far off in all the countries to which You have driven them, because of the unfaithfulness which they have committed against You.

"O Lord, to us belongs shame of face, to our kings, our princes, and our fathers, because we have sinned against You. To the Lord our God belong mercy and forgiveness, though we have rebelled against Him. We have not obeyed the voice of the LORD our God, to walk in His laws, which He set before us by His servants the prophets.

Daniel 9:4-10

I'm convinced that we're about to witness the most powerful move of God this nation has ever experienced. Unfortunately, many, including Christians, will be oblivious to it or will choose to ignore it.

Although we're still in the early stages of it, we're already seeing a separation taking place between the lukewarm, politically correct social "church" and the true church of Jesus Christ. The first is a totally man-made religious entity which Paul describes as one having a "form of godliness but denying its power" (2 Timothy 3:5). The other being the faithful, uncompromising church that will persevere until the return of Jesus Christ. The Bible also mentions this church in the following way:

They overcame him by the blood of the Lamb and by the word of their testimony, and they did not love their lives to the death.

Revelation 12:11

As you're reading this book, you may be going through some serious personal difficulty. By no means do I want to minimize the importance of your situation. But I want to encourage you in the Lord, not to submit to this difficulty and thus lose sight of the big picture. Don't forget that you are living during the period of human history Paul describes as "perilous times". What you're going through may be an attack whose purpose is to distract you from your primary assignment. God did not make a mistake. He knew perfectly well what kind of environment you'd be living in. But He also made provision for you to triumph over those adverse conditions and for you to fulfill your assignment victoriously!

MAKING A DISTINCTION

Even after being told that God was about to take them out of Egypt, the children of Israel continued to live in that adverse environment. As God's judgment was executed on this evil nation, His people were protected through the entire process.

I will set apart the land of Goshen, in which My people dwell, that no swarms of flies shall be there, in order that you may know that I am the LORD in the midst of the land. I will make a difference between My people and your people.

Exodus 8:22-23

Judgment is coming on the nations of the world and I don't believe that America will be spared. Not only will the true people of God will be protected during this time, but I believe that they'll be blessed and prosper in a greater way than ever before!

FIGHTING FOR AMERICA

Just as important as it is for us to recognize who the real enemies of America are, we also need to know how to fight against them.

As long as the focus of our attention remains on what we perceive to be natural adversaries, not only will we have limited power against them, but there is no guarantee that God will grant us victory over them.

For we do not wrestle against flesh and blood, but against principalities, against powers, against the rulers of the darkness of this age, against spiritual hosts of wickedness in the heavenly places.

Ephesians 6 :12

The fight for America I'm talking about, is not political, military or philosophical. Far too many people believe that what we need to protect the most in this country, is the notion that we're a democracy.

Just as important as it was for the children of Israel to be in Goshen to benefit from God's protection, I'm convinced that we need to be in churches that preach the uncompromised word of God and do not conform to this present system or environment.

If you're currently in a "church" that is more interested in gathering crowds than in preparing God's people for the times we live in and is failing to challenge you in accomplishing your destiny, I urge you to join a true church as fast as you possibly can!

If My people who are called by My name will humble themselves, and pray and seek My face, and turn from their wicked ways, then I will hear from heaven, and will forgive their sin and heal their land.

2 Chronicles 7:14

It is high time for God's people in America to rediscover their true identity in Christ. Whether you were born here or if like me you came from elsewhere, what makes you an American has little or nothing to do with where you were born. I believe it has everything to do with one's willingness to embrace and participate in the vision of this beloved country.

CONCLUSION

I first want to thank you for taking the time to read this book. I pray that I was able to convince you to stand for our beloved America as you never have before. No matter what your level of involvement might have been up to this point, I encourage you to engage in the political process of this nation, at the very minimum, by voting responsibly and according to your conscience.

If you are a Christian, understand that God has put you on the earth for a special purpose. You're not here by accident, nor where you born at this particular time of history by chance. I believe that God has called you and me to America for such a time as this. No matter what the focus of our attention might have been in the past, it is urgent for all believers to recognize that God has ordained us to play an important part in these end times. He has granted us power, authority and favor, to overcome the forces of evil that have been raised against this nation.

I have nothing against people purchasing weapons and ammunition in anticipation of things to come. But there's so much more we can do, beside just protecting ourselves. Strategic, offensive attacks on an enemy, are the best form of defense. Our effective, fervent prayer is the most powerful weapon in a believer's arsenal!

Like queen Esther, we might come up with all sorts of excuses for not fighting in what I believe to be the greatest threat America has ever faced. God will not do for the Church what He has commissioned the Church to do!

Humanly, it would seem as though we're powerless against the enemy's attacks, but remember that things that are impossible with men, are possible with God. If He is for us, the Bible says, who can be against us.

This thought has probably come to you, as it has to me: "what can I do? I'm only one person against so many!" Its true that we're very limited as individual believers... But you're not alone! Listen to the words of Jesus:

"Again I say to you that if two of you agree on earth concerning anything that they ask, it will be done for them by My Father in heaven."

Matt 18:19-20

I believe that the time has come for Christians of diverse backgrounds and persuasions to put aside their differences and unite around the common cause of defending our nation. This war will not be won with conventional weapons or political might, but through the united and focused prayers of Christian men and women who truly care about America.

If we mobilize enough believers in the fight against the enemies of this wonderful nation, you and I won't be wondering any longer "O America where art thou". But we'll rediscover the country God intended it to be and, without hesitation or embarrassment, we'll be able to sing: "America, God has indeed shed His grace on Thee!

CREDITS

HARRY TRUMAN
www.presidency.ucsb.edu/ws/index.php?pid=13707

MAYFLOWER COMPACT -From the *History of Plymouth Plantation* by William Bradford (1590-1657), second governor of Plymouth.

THE DECLARATION OF INDEPENDENCE – U.S. National Archives & Administration - www.archives.gov

THE HISTORY OF AMERICA – By Noah Webster
https://www.**noahwebster**house.org/.../**noah**-**webster**-history.htm

EDMUND BURKE Quote
http://www.brainyquote.com/quotes/authors/e/edmund_burke.html

PRESIDENT RONALD REAGAN ON THE BIBLE
Ronald Reagan Presidential Library, National Archives and Records Administration

THE MAYFLOWER COMPACT -From the *History of Plymouth Plantation* by William Bradford (1590- 1657), second governor of Plymouth.

BENJAMIN HARRISON – 23rd President of the United States
http:/www.presidentbenjaminharrisson.org/learn/Benjamin-harrisson-1/president

COMMUNIST GOALS – NAKED COMMUNIST by Cleon Skousen
1963 Congressional Record

Dr. RICHARD LEE – Dignity of Human Life
The American Patriot's Bible

Dr. RICHARD LEE – Principles of Judeo-Christian Ethics
The American Patriot's Bible

MARGARET SANGER – On page 108 of the Birth Control Review of April 1932

First Amendment Religion Clauses: RHODE ISLAND CHARTER (1683) and Constitution (1842)

PRESIDENT ANDREW JACKSON - Excerpt from his Farewell address - 1837

ISBN-13: 978-1517299354

ISBN-10: 1517299357

OTHER BOOKS

by Rev. Jean-Paul Engler

THE UNHOLY ALLIANCE – A book that exposes the end-time strategy of three major spiritual entities bent on the destruction of Israel, America and the Church of Jesus-Christ.

GRACE ANATOMY – Not only does this book expose the heretical teaching of the hyper grace message, but it provides the reader with the scriptural knowledge to defuse the damaging effects of that teaching and the needed equipping to rescue those who've been infected by it.

FAITH THAT ACTUALLY WORKS – Presents the subject of faith in a fresh and uncomplicated way.

THE WINNING CHURCH – Jesus is coming back for a Church that fits a criteria He has established in His Word. This book explains what this criteria is, how we currently measure up to it and what we must do to meet it.

L'EGLISE QUI GAGNE – A French translation of the WINNING CHURCH book by the same author.

LA FOI QUI FONCTIONNE VRAIMENT - A French translation of the FAITH THAT ACTUALLY WORKS book by the same author.

These books are available on Amazon in both printed form and digital. They can also be ordered directly, by contacting FSCO – PO Box 423- NEW MARKET, TN 37820 or fscoevei@aol.com

Volume discounts are available

Made in the USA
Columbia, SC
07 May 2021